SandCastle™

Let's Measure More

WHAT IN THE WORLD IS A LEAP YEAR?

AND OTHER TIME MEASUREMENTS

A Division of ABDO

ABDO
Publishing Company

Desirée Bussiere

Consulting Editor, Diane Craig, M.A./Reading Specialist

visit us at www.abdopublishing.com

Published by ABDO Publishing Company, a division of ABDO, P.O. Box 398166, Minneapolis, Minnesota 55439. Copyright © 2013 by Abdo Consulting Group, Inc. International copyrights reserved in all countries. No part of this book may be reproduced in any form without written permission from the publisher. SandCastle™ is a trademark and logo of ABDO Publishing Company.

Printed in the United States of America, North Mankato, Minnesota
102012
082013

 PRINTED ON RECYCLED PAPER

Editor: Liz Salzmann
Content Developer: Nancy Tuminelly
Cover and Interior Design: Colleen Dolphin, Mighty Media, Inc.
Cover and Interior Production: Kate Hartman
Photo Credits: Shutterstock

Library of Congress Cataloging-in-Publication Data

Bussierre, Desireé, 1989- author.
 What in the world is a leap year? : and other time measurements / Desireé Bussierre ; consulting editor, Diane Craig, M.A./reading specialist.
      pages cm. -- (Let's measure more)
Audience: 4-9
ISBN 978-1-61783-597-1
1. Time--Juvenile literature. 2. Leap year--Juvenile literature. I. Title.
QB209.5.B88 2013
529'.2--dc23

                                      2012025986

SandCastle™ Level: Transitional

SandCastle™ books are created by a team of professional educators, reading specialists, and content developers around five essential components—phonemic awareness, phonics, vocabulary, text comprehension, and fluency—to assist young readers as they develop reading skills and strategies and increase their general knowledge. All books are written, reviewed, and leveled for guided reading, early reading intervention, and Accelerated Reader® programs for use in shared, guided, and independent reading and writing activities to support a balanced approach to literacy instruction. The SandCastle™ series has four levels that correspond to early literacy development. The levels are provided to help teachers and parents select appropriate books for young readers.

Emerging Readers	Beginning Readers	Transitional Readers	Fluent Readers
(no flags)	(1 flag)	(2 flags)	(3 flags)

contents

Time is how long something takes. Time is measured in seconds, minutes, hours, days, and years.

We use clocks and watches to tell time. They show the seconds, minutes, and hours.

One hour has 60 minutes. One minute has 60 seconds.

time?

Jake has a new watch. He wears it every day. His watch says it is 3:45.

The Earth spins constantly. A day is how long it takes to spin around one time. There are 24 hours in a day.

Each day starts at midnight. Midnight is at 12:00 **a.m.** The middle of the day is noon. Noon is at 12:00 **p.m.**

a day?

Ryan wakes up at 7:00 **a.m.** He goes to bed at 8:30 **p.m.**

What is

The Earth moves around the sun. A year is how long it takes to go around once. You can use a calendar to measure a year.

One year has 12 months. One month has about 4 weeks. One week has 7 days.

a year?

APRIL

SUNDAY	MONDAY	TUESDAY	WEDNESDAY	THURSDAY	FRIDAY	
						2
						ballet class
						9
		ballet class	6	ballet class 7		ballet class 16
3	4	5				
		ballet class	13	ballet class 14		ballet class 23
10	11	12				
		ballet class	20	ballet class 21		ballet class
17	18	19				
		ballet class	27	ballet class 28		
24	25	26				

Lily loves to dance! She has **ballet** class three days each week. She writes it on her calendar.

What is a

A decade is 10 years. A decade is often called by its first year. The 1990s is a decade. It is the time from 1990 to 2000.

decade?

Ethan's grandpa is 70 years old. He has lived for seven decades!

A century is 100 years.
The United States turned
100 years old in 1876.
There was a huge fair in
Philadelphia! It was called
the Centennial Exposition.

century?

Ella listens to a **phonograph**. It is more than a century old.

What is a

A millennium is one thousand years. Very few things last that long. The Tower of London is almost a millennium old. It was built in 1078.

millennium?

The third millennium began in 2000. Luke's family had a big party. They wore colorful hats.

An eon is one **billion** years. Scientists use eons to measure the time since Earth began. Earth is four and one-half eons old!

an eon?

Mia learns about dinosaurs. They lived a very long time ago. But it was the same eon we live in now!

A fortnight is fourteen days. The word *fortnight* is not used very often in the United States.

Fortnight is also used in **astronomy**. It is the time between a full moon and a new moon. A full moon looks completely round. A new moon is when you can't see the moon at all.

fortnight?

Tonight is a full moon. Owen counts ahead fourteen days. That's when there will be a new moon. It will be extra dark that night.

SUNDAY	MONDAY	TUESDA				TURDAY
						2
3	4 Full Moon	5	6	7	8	9
10	11	12	13	14	15	16
17	18 New Moon	19	20	21	22	23
24	25	26	27	28	29	30

A leap year has one extra day. It happens every four years. A regular year has 365 days. A leap year has 366 days. The extra day is February 29. It is called *leap day*.

leap year?

Emily was born on leap day. She usually **celebrates** her birthday on February 28th. In a leap year, she can celebrate on her real birthday!

Fun facts

⇨ About one out of every 1,500 people is born on leap day.

⇨ The **sundial** was one of the first kinds of clocks.

⇨ In 1582, **Pope** Gregory XIII told people to use a new calendar to measure the year. This calendar was named after him. It is called the Gregorian calendar. Today, most countries around the world use the Gregorian calendar.

⇨ Eon can also be spelled *aeon*.

Quiz

Read each sentence below. Then decide whether it is true or false.

1. The Earth spins constantly. True or False?

2. One year has 12 months. True or False?

3. There are 10 years in a century. True or False?

4. A leap year has 366 days. True or False?

5. The word *fortnight* is used in **astronomy**. True or False?

Glossary

a.m. — short for *ante meridiem*, which is Latin for *before noon*.

astronomy — the study of outer space, such as planets, moons, and stars.

ballet — a type of dance that tells a story.

billion — a very large number. One billion is also written 1,000,000,000.

celebrate — to honor with a party or special ceremony.

p.m. — short for *post meridiem*, which is Latin for *after noon*.

phonograph — a machine that plays sounds from a record.

pope — the leader of the Roman Catholic Church.

sundial — a tool for telling time. It has a rod sticking up from a flat surface. As the sun moves, the rod's shadow points to the time.